I Was Wondering That, Too!

Aaron Erhardt

Erhardt Publications
Louisville, Kentucky
2015

Dedication

Johnna Heitz

I could not ask for a better mother-in-law.
She has a servant's heart and a tender soul.

Table of Contents

Introduction	1
Is Being Good, Good Enough?	3
Does It Make a Difference What One Believes?	13
How Is One Saved By Grace?	23
Has the Kingdom Been Established?	31
Is the Bible from God?	41
Can a Child of God Fall from Grace?	49
How Can I Find the New Testament Church?	59
What Is Church Discipline?	65

Introduction

Four men were on an airplane that began having engine problems. The passengers included a pilot, a professor, a preacher, and a Boy Scout. As the plane lost altitude, the pilot said, "We are going to crash, and there are only three parachutes. Somebody is not going to be able to get out. I have a family and they depend on me, so I'm going to leave." He grabbed a parachute and jumped out.

The professor said, "I am the smartest man in the world. It would be an incalculable loss to society for me to die, so I'm leaving." He grabbed a parachute and jumped out.

The preacher turned to the Boy Scout and said, "Son, I know the Lord and have absolute confidence in my salvation. You've got your whole life in front of you, so you go ahead and take the last parachute."

The Boy Scout said, "No problem, preacher; the smartest man in the world just grabbed my knapsack and jumped out. Here, have a parachute."

The world is full of smart people who foolishly trust "knapsacks" to save them. It might be the knapsack of popular opinion, or the knapsack of personal preference, or the knapsack of family tradition, or the knapsack of my preacher says. They fail to realize that the only device truly capable of providing safety is God's Word (James 1:21). It is our parachute!

With that said, there are many questions that sincere people wonder about, like "Is being good, good enough?" "Does it make a difference what one believes?" and "How is one saved by grace?" These important inquiries and others are answered in this book by "The Book." All else aside, we are relying on the parachute of truth for insight and understanding in these areas. Are you ready to jump?

Is Being Good, Good Enough?

When I was a child, my parents would sometimes watch the television game show *"Family Feud."* Contestants had to name the most popular responses to a question posed to 100 people in order to win cash and prizes. The host would say something like, "The top 7 answers are on the board. We asked 100 people..." Does that ring a bell?

If 100 people were asked to name the one word most often used to describe the deceased person at a funeral, what would it be? My guess would be "good." — He was a "good" man. He was a "good" neighbor. He was a "good" father. He was a "good" friend. He was a "good" employee. — The one word you hear over and over is that the deceased person was "good." And most of the time, there is a lot of truth to that assessment.

The world is full of good people. They work hard, help others, and behave properly. They make an honest living, donate to charities, coach little league baseball teams, cut their elderly-neighbor's lawn, and tip generously at restaurants. They are dependable and trustworthy. They are good people.

Examples

I recently read about a woman, now 88, who found 30 abandoned Chinese babies on the roadside. She gathered up those babies and cared for them, even though her only means of support was recycling rubbish.

A kid was shopping with his mother and asked her to buy him a new bike, for his had recently been stolen. His mother told him that she could not afford to purchase a new bike. Then a large man covered in tattoos walked over and handed the boy $350. He said, "No child should ever be without a bike in the summer."

During WWII, a lady named Irena received permission to work as a plumbing specialist in the

Warsaw Ghetto. However, she had an ulterior motive. Irena used her tool box and a sack to smuggle out Jewish infants. She even trained her dog to bark around Nazi soldiers to drown out any noises the infants might make. Irena smuggled out 2,500 children, though she was eventually caught and had her arms and legs broken.

A teenager chased a car on his bike for 15 minutes to save a little girl who had been kidnapped from her front yard in Pennsylvania. Because of his relentlessness, the kidnapper finally pulled over and let her out.

These four examples, along with countless others that could be mentioned, demonstrate that there are good people in the world. They look out for others, go the extra mile, and act in ways that are praiseworthy. But is being good, good enough?

Clarification

Before we answer that question, let me clarify my use of the word "good." I recognize that no one is "good" in an absolute sense (Ecclesiastes 7:20;

Romans 3:23). However, the Bible does speak of "good" people. Paul wrote,

> "For one will scarcely die for a righteous person — though perhaps for a good person one would dare even to die" (Romans 5:7).

You may recall that Joseph of Arimathea was described as a "good" man in Luke 23:50; Barnabas was called a "good" man in Acts 11:24; and Proverbs speaks of a "good" man (12:2; 14:14). Furthermore, older women are to teach younger women to be "good" (Titus 2:5, YLT). Now back to our question.

Is Being Good, Good Enough?

Many people answer that question in the affirmative. They think that all good people go to heaven. Regardless of a person's religious convictions, so long as they have some sense of decency and morality about them, they will be saved. However, the Scriptural answer to that question is "no."

Before we look at biblical examples of "good" people who still needed to be saved, let me impress upon you the consequences of this idea. If being good is good enough, then we don't need God's grace, Christ's sacrifice, the church's existence, or the gospel's power. If good is good enough, those things are not necessary. Now let's look at some examples.

1. *Cornelius.* He was described by the Holy Spirit as "a devout man who feared God with all his household, gave alms generously to the people, and prayed continually to God" (Acts 10:2). Even his men spoke highly of him. They said that Cornelius was "an upright and God-fearing man, who is well spoken of by the whole Jewish nation" (v. 22). Here was a man who was pious, charitable, prayerful, and highly regarded. Yet he still needed to be saved (Acts 11:14).

2. *Eunuch.* He was described as "a court official of Candace, queen of the Ethiopians, who was in charge of all her treasure" (Acts 8:27). This implies that the eunuch was a man of great

integrity, for the queen would never appoint an untrustworthy person to such an important position. If he had a shady reputation or was suspicious, sneaky, and sly, the eunuch would never have been made treasurer. Moreover, he had "come to Jerusalem to worship" and was on his way home "reading the prophet Isaiah" (vv. 27-28). Hence, he was a very religious person who traveled a great distance to serve God and was still reading his Bible as he returned. The eunuch was also a humble person, for no prideful person would ask a stranger to help him understand the Scriptures. Yet he still needed to be saved (vv. 35-39).

3. *Rich young man.* He was a zealous keeper of the Law who was interested in spiritual things. In fact, he came running to Jesus and knelt before Him to ask a question about eternal life (Mark 10:17). When Jesus said, "You know the commandments: Do not murder, Do not commit adultery, Do not steal, Do not bear false witness, Do

not defraud, Honor your father and mother" (v. 19), the man replied, "Teacher, all these I have kept from my youth" (v. 20). Obviously, he was a good person. He had kept the commandments since childhood. Yet he was "disheartened" and "went away sorrowful" when Jesus pointed out his weakness (v. 22).

There are other examples we could consider. For instance, Jesus said that some at Judgment will stand before Him having done many good things; yet they will be lost (Matt. 7:21-23). Furthermore, the Jews on Pentecost were described as "devout men" (Acts 2:5). One translation says, "They were good men who believed in God" (WE). They were decent, pious people. However, they still needed to be saved (v. 40).

Extras

1. *"Good" is a relative term.* Our perception of "good" is often subjective. It may vary from one person or group to

another. An example of this is Saul of Tarsus. He was considered "good" to the Jews, though he was anything but "good" in the sight of Christians.

2. *Some are too good.* There are people who put so much trust in their own perceived goodness that they have no need for the church or the gospel. "I am good enough already," they think. Hence, they are "too good" to be saved.

3. *Goodness is absolutely necessary.* We do not want to diminish the importance of being good. One simply cannot be a good Christian without being a good person (3 John 11).

Conclusion

The world is full of good people. They can be found in every denomination and in every world religion. They can even be found among those who have no religious affiliation at all. However, the Scriptures are clear that being good is not good enough. One must obey the gospel and faithfully serve God to have eternal life.

good - used many times throughout the Bible

I Was Wondering That, Too!

Does It Make a Difference What One Believes?

Does it make a difference what one believes? I think we would all agree that it does make a difference in certain situations. For instance, a man in Michigan believed he was shooting a coyote, but it was actually a woman's dog. He was arrested and charged with careless discharge of a firearm and property damage over $50. A man in New York believed he was shooting a deer, but it was actually a hunter. He was arrested and charged with second-degree murder. A cop in Florida believed he was arresting a teenager who had sexually-assaulted a young girl, but he was actually a different teenager with the same name. The boy spent 35 days in jail as a result. In situations like these, it obviously makes a difference what one believes.

Now let's get more specific. *Does it make a difference what one believes in religious matters?* Many people today have embraced the idea that as long as you "accept Jesus" it does not matter what you believe otherwise. You may believe in tongue speaking, Sabbath keeping, baby sprinkling, incense burning, relic bowing, gay marrying, dead raising or whatever you want. It doesn't make a difference. You can "join the church of your choice" and take the path to heaven that best suits you. Max Lucado put it like this:

> "Well, the best I can figure it, the situation looks something like this. God has enlisted us into His navy. We have been called to serve on a ship… There are those aboard this ship who say once you get on it, you're never able to get off no matter what you do. And then there are others — equally serious students — who say to get off would be foolish and fatal, but the choice is always yours. There are those, I have noticed, on this

ship who say you are here out of no choice of your own, you were predestined to be a sailor; not everyone was, but you were. And then there are those who say, no, God is a God of choice and He would only leave that choice with us. There are those who say that before this ship docks, there will be a great and mighty tribulation. There are those who say, yes, there will be a great and mighty tribulation, but that will come after this ship safely reaches the shore. And, oh, how we tend to cluster. And then there is the matter of the weekly meeting in which we gather to read the words of the Captain and give thanks to Him. We all agree that it is necessary, but that's about the extent of our agreement. There are those who say it should be solemn; there are those who say it should be spontaneous. There are those who say certain genders should be quiet; there are those who say certain genders should be loud. There are those who say we should play the trumpet and then there are those who say, no, my voice is simply trumpet enough. And, oh, how we tend to cluster" (1995 Pepperdine University Bible Lectures, Max Lucado, quoted from *Piloting the Strait*, pp. 318-320).

Notice how Lucado includes all the different denominational groups on this ship. It does not matter to him if you are a Calvinist, Premillennialist, or Pentecostal. He readily accepts women preachers and instrumental music, too. Obviously, Lucado does not think it makes a difference what one believes in religious matters. And so it is with many others.

What Does the Bible Say?

The Bible says that what one believes *does* make a difference in religious matters. We must "believe the truth" (2 Thessalonians 2:12; also 1 Timothy 4:3). That includes everything taught in the New Testament. We are also warned that those who do not abide in the truth "do not have God" (2 John 9). How then can anyone say that it doesn't matter what one believes?

In Ephesians 4, Paul listed the "seven ones" of Christian unity. Among them was "one faith" (v. 5). That means there is only one system of beliefs, or body of truth, that is right in the sight of God. If that is true, then it makes a difference what one believes.

If it makes no difference what one believes in religious matters, why did Paul emphasize the need for "soundness" so much? He spoke of "sound words" (2 Timothy 1:13), "sound teaching" (2 Timothy 4:3), "sound doctrine" (Titus 2:1), "sound in faith" (Titus 2:2) etc. The Greek word for "sound" is *hygianousei*, from which we get our English word "hygiene." It means to be of good health. It is used by Paul in reference to that which is correct or true. Obviously, he believed that "doctrinal matters matter!"

I am reminded of the story of the young prophet in 1 Kings 13. He was commanded by God to go and prophesy against King Jeroboam's altar, which he did admirably. However, on his way home an older prophet deceived him into believing a lie and he perished.

"Now an old prophet lived in Bethel. And his sons came and told him all that the man of God had done that day in Bethel. They also told to their father the words that he had spoken to the king. And their father said to them, 'Which way did he go?' And his sons showed him the way that the man of God who came from Judah had gone. And he said to his sons, 'Saddle the donkey for me.' So they saddled the donkey for him and he mounted it. And he went after the man of God and found him sitting under an oak. And he said to him, 'Are you the man of God who came from Judah?' And he said, 'I am.' Then he said to him, 'Come home with me and eat bread.' And he said, 'I may not return with you, or go in with you, neither will I eat bread nor drink water with you in this place, for it was said to me by the word of the Lord, You shall neither eat bread nor drink water there, nor return by the way that you came.' And he said to him, 'I also am a prophet as you are, and an angel spoke to me by the word of the

Lord, saying, Bring him back with you into your house that he may eat bread and drink water.' But he lied to him. So he went back with him and ate bread in his house and drank water. And as they sat at the table, the word of the Lord came to the prophet who had brought him back. And he cried to the man of God who came from Judah, 'Thus says the Lord, Because you have disobeyed the word of the Lord and have not kept the command that the Lord your God commanded you, but have come back and have eaten bread and drunk water in the place of which he said to you, Eat no bread and drink no water, your body shall not come to the tomb of your fathers.' And after he had eaten bread and drunk, he saddled the donkey for the prophet whom he had brought back. And as he went away a lion met him on the road and killed him. And his body was thrown in the road, and the donkey stood beside it; the lion also stood beside the body. And behold, men passed by and saw the body thrown in the road and the lion standing by the body. And they came and told it in the city where the old prophet lived" (vv. 11-25).

Notice that the young prophet believed a lie. He believed that an angel brought new revelation to the older prophet allowing him to do what God had forbidden. Did that make any difference? Undoubtedly it did! He was killed by a lion as he made his way home. This story should forever silence those who say that it doesn't matter what you believe.

Consequences

This idea is certainly one of the devil's best achievements. If he can convince people that it does not make a difference what they believe, they won't even try to closely follow God's Word or contend with others over important doctrinal matters. And those who insist on "sound doctrine" will be scoffed at and labeled "extreme" by the populace. Indeed, we are already seeing that to be the case.

Conclusion

Jesus and the inspired writers taught that there is an objective standard by which we shall be judged (John 12:48; Romans 2:16; James 2:12). We must comply with that standard to be saved. Hence, it does make a difference what we believe.

How Is One Saved By Grace?

On August 5, 2010, a group of Chilean miners found themselves trapped nearly half a mile beneath the surface of the earth. They were buried under 2,300 feet of rock with very little food, water, and oxygen. And it was not just for a few seconds, or minutes, or hours. They were trapped for 69 agonizing days before finally being lifted out one by one in a specially-designed capsule.

Those miners knew they needed help. They were cut off from above, buried 2,300 feet deep, and unable to do anything about it on their own. They had to rely on outside intervention. And when help finally presented itself in the form of a capsule, they were eager to get inside and remain there until it reached the top.

The rescue of the Chilean miners perfectly illustrates the concept of salvation by grace. Man is cut off from above, buried deep in sin, and unable to do anything about it on his own. He must rely on outside intervention, which has come in the form of Jesus Christ. He is the saving capsule! However, man must get "into" Him (Galatians 3:27) and "remain" there (John 15:4, NIV) to reach the top. Do you see the parallel?

Grace: What?

"Grace" is unmerited favor or undeserved blessing. It comes from the Greek word *charis*, and is often used in the New Testament of the favor God bestows on sinners through Jesus Christ. Perhaps the biblical concept of grace can be summed up as "not receiving what we deserve and not deserving what we receive."

By grace, God did for us what we could not do for ourselves. He made a way of salvation through Christ (Romans 3:24-25; John 3:16; 1 John 4:9-10). This is what makes grace so amazing! God's goodness toward us was not based on any goodness we had done or would do in the future. He acted freely and without expectation of receiving anything of equitable value in return. It was unearned kindness!

Before we can truly appreciate grace, we must come to grips with the depth of our sins. Our sins separate us from God (Isaiah 59:1-2). Paul said that "all have sinned and fall short of the glory of God" (Romans 3:23) and that "the wages of sin is death" (Romans 6:23). This means that each of us deserve eternal separation from God in hell. It is the appropriate "payoff" (NET). Yet God graciously made provisions to rid us of the horrifying clutches of sin and save us from such misery (Romans 5:8).

Grace: Who?

By grace, Jesus died "for all" (2 Corinthians 5:14). He tasted death "for everyone" (Hebrews 2:9). He is the propitiation "for the sins of the whole world" (1 John 2:2). This means that all can benefit from what God has done through Christ. None are beyond reach! Perhaps this is best seen in the life of Paul. He said to King Agrippa,

> "I myself was convinced that I ought to do many things in opposing the name of Jesus of Nazareth. And I did so in Jerusalem. I not only locked up many of the saints in prison after receiving authority from the chief priests, but when they were put to death I cast my vote against them. And punished them often in all the synagogues and tried to make them blaspheme, and in raging fury against them I persecuted them even to foreign cities" (Acts 26:9-11).

Yet he was later saved. If Paul could receive grace when judgment was long overdue, anyone can (1 Timothy 1:16).

Another example is much more recent. Jeffrey Dahmer was one of the most notorious serial killers in American history. He was sentenced to 15 consecutive life terms for the rape, murder, and dismemberment of 17 males between 1978 and 1991. Some of the murders involved cannibalism. Yet he learned the truth and was baptized into Christ shortly before he was beaten to death on November

28, 1994. Below is an excerpt from Roy Ratcliff, the preacher who did the baptism:

> "Nearly everyone raises the question about Jeff's sincerity. But I was there, and these questioners weren't... I cannot know the condition of another person's heart unless I listen to his or her words. I listened to Jeff's words, and I watched his eyes and his body language. I listened to the tone of his voice and observed his mannerisms, and I am convinced that he was totally sincere in his desire... Jeff had nothing to gain in this life by being baptized; he had everything to gain in the next life. He was baptized for the same reason anyone else is baptized. In the light of the Bible, he surveyed his life and concluded that he needed to be saved" (*The Baptism of Jeffrey Dahmer*, Roy Ratcliff, Christian Woman, 1995).

If Paul was the "foremost" sinner of the first century (1 Timothy 1:15), Jeffrey Dahmer was certainly among the "foremost" sinners of the twentieth century. However, neither man was beyond the scope of God's grace!

David once declared, "When I look at your heavens, the work of your fingers, the moon and the stars, which you have set in place, what is man that you are mindful of him, and the sons of man that you care for him" (Psalm 8:3-4)? It is truly amazing to know that God is interested in us, as weak and wretched as we are, and that He cared enough to send His Son into the world to die as a sacrifice for sin. Who then are we to arbitrarily choose who is and is not "worthy" of such grace? If God extended His grace to all who will accept it, shouldn't we do the same?

Grace: How?

Though salvation is by grace, it is not by grace alone. Paul said that we are saved "by grace...through faith" (Ephesians 2:8). Grace is God's part; faith is man's part. If salvation were by grace alone, then all would be saved since "the grace of God has appeared, bringing salvation for all people" (Titus 2:11). Yet we know that not all will be saved (Matthew 7:13-14). Hence, grace is appropriated conditionally.

There are many examples of grace being appropriated conditionally in Scripture. For instance, Noah was saved from the flood by grace *when* he built the ark (Genesis 6), the Israelites were healed of snakebite by grace *when* they looked at the bronze serpent (Numbers 21), the Israelites conquered Jericho by grace *when* they marched around the walls (Joshua 6), Naaman was healed of leprosy by grace *when* he dipped in the Jordan (2 Kings 5), and the Jews on Pentecost were forgiven of their sins by grace *when* they repented and were baptized (Acts 2). In each of these cases, a lack of human cooperation would have thwarted God's grace.

The household of Cornelius heard, believed, repented, and were baptized (Acts 15:7; 11:18; 10:48). Then Peter said they were saved by grace (Acts 15:11). The same is true with the Ephesians. They heard, believed, repented, and were baptized (Ephesians 1:13; Acts 20:31; 19:5). Then Paul said they were saved by grace (Ephesians 2:8). Thus we see that salvation by grace involves an obedient faith on the part of man.

Conclusion

It is impossible for man to save himself. He cannot work long enough, hard enough, or good enough to remove the guilt of sin and earn a home in heaven. He must rely on God's grace. Though grace is a gift that is available to all, it is not accepted by all. If you have not experienced the "amazing grace" of God, you can do it through an obedient faith (Mark 16:16; Acts 2:38; Romans 10:9-10). Those Chilean miners took advantage of the opportunity to be made free, why not do the same?

Has the Kingdom Been Established?

Many in the religious world, commonly known as Premillennialists, teach that the kingdom is not currently in existence. They say that although Christ intended to set up the kingdom while on earth the first time, He was crucified before He could do it. W.E. Blackstone put it like this:

> "This Kingdom was at hand, that is, it came nigh (or approached, same Greek word), when Jesus, the King, came. So much so, that the three favored disciples witnessed a foretaste of its glory and power on the Mount of Transfiguration. But the Jews rejected it and slew their King. They were not willing to have this man reign over them, and therefore the Kingdom did not 'immediately appear'…

> The Kingdom did come 'nigh' when Christ came, and had they received Him, it would have been manifested, but now it is in abeyance, or waiting until He comes again" (*Jesus is Coming*, W.E. Blackstone, ch. 10).

As you can see, those who subscribe to this doctrine believe that Jesus was stopped from setting up His kingdom as planned because of Jewish opposition. Therefore, it had to be delayed or "sovereignly postponed" (*Matthew 1-7*, John McArthur, p. 56). But is that true?

Kingdom in Prophecy

In Daniel 2, King Nebuchadnezzar had a dream that troubled him. When the wise men of the nation could not interpret the dream he ordered them to be slain. Daniel, however, a prophet of God, volunteered to interpret it. He said, "You saw, O king, and behold, a great image. This image, mighty and of exceeding brightness, stood before you, and its appearance was frightening" (v. 31). He then went on to describe the image and what it represented.

The sections of the image represented four consecutive world-ruling empires. The first was Babylonia (626-539), then Medo-Persia (539-330), then Greece (330-63), and finally Rome (63+). Daniel then declared, "And in the days of those kings the God of heaven will set up a kingdom that shall never be destroyed, nor shall the kingdom be left to another people. It shall break in pieces all these kingdoms and bring them to an end, and it shall stand forever" (v. 44). Hence, the kingdom would be established during the Roman Empire's rule.

In Daniel 7, we are told that the kingdom would be given to the Lord when going to the Ancient of Days in heaven (vv. 13-14). Obviously, that refers to the time of the ascension. "There should be no argument as to whom or what this scene referred. Daniel spoke from heaven's point of view. He was describing the return of God's Son, as the Son of man and the Son of God, when He received the promised kingdom from His Father. And Luke, speaking from earth's point of view, described the same event in the first two chapters of Acts" (*A Commentary on Daniel*, Homer Hailey, p. 140).

Kingdom in Promise

When we reach the gospel accounts, Rome was the world-ruling empire. It was time for Daniel's prophecy to be fulfilled. It is no wonder then that John the Baptist and Jesus declared that the kingdom was "at hand" (Matthew 3:2; Mark 1:15). In fact, Jesus promised that it would be established during that generation. He said, "Truly, I say to you, there are some standing here who will not taste death until they see the kingdom of God after it has come with power" (Mark 9:1). Thus, the stage was set for the ushering in of the kingdom.

Kingdom in Fulfillment

The kingdom was indeed established in the first century. There are many passages that prove this point. Consider the following.

> **Colossians 1:13** — "He has delivered us from the domain of darkness and transferred us to the kingdom of his beloved Son."

Hebrews 12:28 — "Therefore let us be grateful for receiving a kingdom that cannot be shaken, and thus let us offer to God acceptable worship, with reverence and awe."

Revelation 1:9 — "I John, your brother and partner in the tribulation and the kingdom and the patient endurance that are in Jesus, was on the island called Patmos on account of the word of God and the testimony of Jesus."

Notice that the Colossian brethren were in the kingdom, the Hebrew brethren were in the kingdom, and John the apostle was in the kingdom. How then can anyone teach that the kingdom is not currently in existence?

Kingdom is Coming	Kingdom is Close	Kingdom is Current
"And in the days of these kings shall the God of heaven set up a kingdom, which shall never be destroyed" (Dan. 2:44)	"In those days came John the Baptist, preaching in the wilderness of Judea, and saying, Repent ye: for the kingdom of heaven is at hand" (Matt. 3:1-2)	"Who hath delivered us from the power of darkness, and hath translated us into the kingdom of His dear Son" (Col. 1:13)
Old Testament	Gospels	New Testament

We must understand that the kingdom is spiritual in nature (Luke 17:20-21). It was never intended to be an earthly kingdom, bound by geographical boundaries. It is "not of this world" (John 18:36).

Consequences

There are many harmful consequences for those who deny that the kingdom is in existence. For instance, if there is no kingdom, no one has been converted (Matthew 18:3, KJV), no one has a right to eat the Lord's Supper (Luke 22:18), no one has been born again (John 3:5), and no one has been delivered from the power of darkness (Colossians 1:13). Furthermore, Daniel, John, and Jesus were wrong in their predictions (Daniel 2:44; Matthew 3:2; Mark 1:15; 9:1). Who can believe that?

Premillennialism makes Jesus a failure. It says that He intended to set up the kingdom, but was stopped from doing it. Hence, He was unsuccessful the first time (i.e., He failed)! Premillennialism also makes Him a King without a kingdom. I am convinced that many who have embraced this doctrine did so based solely on emotion, without consulting the Scriptures. I pray they will reconsider their belief. To deny the kingdom's existence is to deny the truth of God's Word!

Kingdom & Church

In many instances, the terms "kingdom" and "church" are used interchangeably in Scripture. They refer to the same institution (Matthew 16:18-19). They share the same origin in date and place, the same territory, the same ownership, and the same requirements for membership. Furthermore, the

Lord's Supper is said to be in both the kingdom (Luke 22:18) and the church (1 Corinthians 11). Premillennialists err when they try to separate the two.

Misapplying Revelation

Premillennialists argue that their doctrine can be sustained in the book of Revelation. However, such is not the case. Revelation is written in apocalyptic language, meaning that much of it is figurative or symbolic. Furthermore, it pertained to things that "must soon take place" (1:1; 22:6). It was not written about activities and events that would transpire just before the Second Coming!

Revelation 20:4 is one of the most frequently used passages by Premillennialists to teach that Jesus will come back to earth, set up a kingdom, and reign for a thousand years. Is that what the passage says? Please note that the passage says nothing about Jerusalem, the Second Coming, Christ stepping foot on the earth, a bodily resurrection, the literal throne of David, or even us. The passage is talking about martyrs! All of those key components must be added (Revelation 22:18).

Conclusion

Premillennialists are wrong. The kingdom was established in the first century as prophesied and promised. It is a spiritual kingdom that will stand forever. Are you a citizen in the kingdom of God?

Is the Bible from God?

The Bible has had an enormous impact on the world. It has influenced cultures and shaped nations. It has been copied and circulated more extensively than any other literature, and has been translated into over two thousand languages. Each day, more than 168,000 Bibles are either sold or given away in the United States.

The Bible claims to be from God. It says, "All Scripture is breathed out by God and profitable for teaching, for reproof, for correction, and for training in righteousness" (2 Timothy 3:16). The phrase "breathed out by God" (*theopneustos*) means that it is the product of His creative breath. This process is best described in 2 Peter 1:21, which says that men "spoke from God as they were carried along by the Holy Spirit." However, claiming to be from God does not prove the point. Many books claim to be from God. How then can we prove that the Bible's claims are true?

Evidence

Unity. The Bible is a library of 66 books. There are 39 books in the Old Testament and 27 books in the New Testament. These books were written over a span of about sixteen hundred years (1500 B.C. — 100 A.D.) by more than forty writers. The writers were not always aware of one another's writings and sometimes did not even know the meaning of their own words (1 Peter 1:10-12). Yet the Bible fits together perfectly. There are no contradictions or inconsistencies.

The writers could hardly have come from more diverse backgrounds. They were shepherds, statesmen, prophets, priests, kings, physicians, fishermen, and tax collectors. They were wealthy and poor, educated and uneducated. They wrote from palaces and prisons, in times of peace and times of war. Furthermore, the Bible was written in three different languages on three different continents.

There is no way that mere men from such diverse backgrounds could have written the Bible in such a unified manner without divine guidance. The unity of the Bible proves that it is from God.

Accuracy. Although the Bible was not written as a textbook on geography, history, or science, it is always accurate in those areas. One of the most fascinating studies of the Bible's accuracy is in the field of archaeology. For instance, Genesis 40 mentions grapes in Egypt. Yet some had contended that the Egyptians never grew grapes or drank wine. However, archaeology has proven that there were grapes in Egypt. Tombs have been discovered which depict the dressing and pruning of vines, and scenes of drunkenness. Another example is the Hittite nation. For a long time critics denied that the Hittites ever existed. However, excavations in Turkey have uncovered their existence.

The ancient Egyptians were renowned for their medical advancements. However, we now know that some of their practices were actually harmful to the patient. For instance, the famous Ebers Papyrus, a medical document of the Egyptians (1552 B.C.), indicates that they would prescribe animal dung in certain instances. This is significant because Moses was "instructed in all the wisdom of the Egyptians" (Acts 7:22), yet he never included any of their harmful practices in his writings. What are the chances that a man educated in the ways of the Egyptians would not incorporate at least some of the faulty remedies of the Egyptians in his writings? Not only that, but every instruction given by Moses has been proven correct by modern medicine. Circumcision on the eighth day, the quarantine of lepers, burning contaminated clothing, burying waste, forbidding the eating of blood, etc. are all proper instructions.

Leviticus 17:11 says, "For the life of the flesh is in the blood." Although we easily understand that statement to be true, until recent times people believed that a sick person needed to have his blood drained. They did not know that blood carries oxygen to the body and removes impurities from it. Yet Moses knew that the blood was life.

The Bible told us that God "hangs the earth on nothing" (Job 26:7) and "sits above the circle of the earth" (Isaiah 40:22) before we knew that the earth hangs from nothing and is round.

Fairness. In most books, there are heroes and villains. The heroes are presented favorably and flawlessly. However, such is not the case with the Bible. It makes no attempts to hide the mistakes of its heroes. For instance, Noah's drunkenness (Genesis 9), Abraham's lies (Genesis 12, 20), Moses' presumption (Numbers 20), David's adultery (2 Samuel 11), and Peter's denials (Matthew 26) are all plainly revealed. There is no attempt to excuse or shield their shortcomings. Human authors tend to present the good side of their heroes. God presents the good, the bad, and the ugly.

Prophecy. The Bible is a book of prophecy. Many of these prophecies were uttered hundreds of years before their fulfillment. For instance, it was prophesied that the Messiah would be born of a virgin (Isaiah 7:14) in the town of Bethlehem (Micah 5:2). It was also prophesied that He would be preceded by a messenger (Isaiah 40:3), betrayed for thirty pieces of silver (Zechariah 11:12-13), pierced in the hands and feet (Psalm 22:16), numbered with the transgressors (Isaiah 53:12), buried in a rich man's tomb (Isaiah 53:9), and resurrected from the dead (Psalm 16:10). All of these prophecies, and countless others, came to pass! Could men utter predications hundreds of years before their fulfillment with such stunning detail without making a mistake? The very thought is absurd. Yet Bible prophecies did just that.

1 Kings 13:2 says, "And the man cried against the altar by the word of the Lord and said, 'O altar, altar, thus says the Lord: Behold, a son shall be born to the house of David, Josiah by name, and he shall sacrifice on you the priests of the high places who make offerings on you, and human bones shall be burned on you.'" This detailed prophecy was fulfilled some 300 years later (2 Kings 23).

Preservation. The Bible has been the object of much persecution. On many occasions men have sought to ban and destroy it, but their efforts have always failed. Others have scrutinized the Bible trying to find contradictions that would prove it false, but to no avail. The Bible has survived the scrutiny. The fact that the Bible continues to exist intact and possess the same strengths today that it has always possessed proves that it is from God.

There is more evidence that proves the Bible is from God. However, these points are more than sufficient. The writers claimed to be inspired (2 Samuel 23:2; 1 Corinthians 14:37; 1 Thessalonians 2:13) and the evidence proves that their claims were true. No other book can do what the Bible does. No other book can pass the tests the Bible passes. The Bible is from God!

The Bible Summed Up		
God made Serpent bade	Plague hit People split	Jesus born Devil scorned
Cain killed Flood filled	Calf erected People infected	Crown worn Veil torn
Abraham went Hagar sent	Spies doubted People pouted	Jesus raised Apostles gazed
Jacob fooled Joseph ruled	Saul freaked David peeked	Church started Spirit imparted
Bush talked Moses balked	Kingdom divided Prophets guided	Word drew Kingdom grew
Jesus is coming	**Jesus is here**	**Jesus is coming again!**

Can a Child of God Fall from Grace?

Many in the religious world, most notably the Calvinists, teach that a child of God can never so sin as to lose his salvation. They say he is "once saved, always saved." The *Westminster Confession of Faith* put it like this:

> "They, whom God has accepted in His Beloved, effectually called, and sanctified by His Spirit, can neither totally nor finally fall away from the state of grace, but shall certainly persevere therein to the end, and be eternally saved" (*Of the Perseverance of the Saints*, 17:1).

The *Baptist Faith and Message* has a similar statement:

> "All true believers endure to the end. Those whom God has accepted in Christ, and sanctified by His Spirit, will never fall away from the state of grace, but shall persevere to the end. Believers may fall into sin through neglect and temptation, whereby they grieve the Spirit, impair their graces and comforts, and bring reproach on the cause of Christ and temporal judgments on themselves; yet they shall be kept by the power of God through faith unto salvation" (Article 5).

A Baptist preacher once took this doctrine to its logical conclusion in a tract entitled *"Do A Christian's Sins Damn His Soul?"* He boldly declared,

> "We take the position that a Christian's sins do not damn his soul. The way a Christian lives, what he says, his character, his conduct, or his attitude toward other people have nothing whatever to do with the salvation of his soul... All the prayers a man may pray, all the Bibles he may read, all the

churches he may belong to, all the services he may attend, all the sermons he may practice, all the debts he may pay, all the ordinances he may observe, all the laws he may keep, all the benevolent acts he may perform will not make his soul one whit safer; and all the sins he may commit from idolatry to murder will not make his soul in any more danger... The way a man lives has nothing whatever to do with the salvation of his soul" (Sam Morris, Stamford, Texas).

Is that true? Is it impossible for a child of God to fall from grace even if he persists in sin? Let's investigate.

Hebrews

The Hebrew brethren were members of the early church. They were called "holy brothers... who share in a heavenly calling" (Hebrews 3:1). There can be no doubt that the writer of the book was in fellowship with those Christians. Yet we see that they could fall away from the living God (3:12), be hardened by the deceitfulness of sin (3:13), fail to reach the promise (4:1), fall by the same sort of disobedience (4:11), spurn the Son of God (10:29), profane the blood of the covenant (10:29), outrage the Spirit of grace (10:29), throw away their confidence (10:35), fail to obtain the grace of God (12:15), become defiled (12:15), refuse Him who speaks from heaven (12:25), etc. Surely no one believes that a person who does those things is still saved.

"If"

The word "if" is a little word with a big meaning. It is a conditional word. If a father tells his son, "I will take you to the movies if you clean your room," we all recognize that the son must meet a condition before going to the movies — he must clean his room. The same is true with our salvation from sin. There are conditions we must meet and maintain. For instance, we are His disciples "if" we abide in His Word (John 8:31), we will be honored "if" we serve Him (John 12:26), we are saved "if" we hold fast to the Word (1 Corinthians 15:1-2), we will reap "if" we do not give up (Galatians 6:9), we are holy "if" we continue in the faith (Colossians 1:22-23), we will never fall "if" we practice certain qualities (2 Peter 1:10), we are cleansed "if" we walk in the light (1 John 1:7), etc. Every honest person can see that there are conditions that a child of God must meet and maintain to be saved. Even the most stubborn soul must concede that "if" is a conditional word.

This is not to say that a child of God has no assurance or confidence. We all believe that he has assurance. In fact, Jesus promised that the believer "does not come into judgment" (John 5:24). However, we must understand that a believer can become an unbeliever. He can develop "an evil, unbelieving heart" (Hebrews 3:12). The blessed assurance of "not coming into judgment" is promised only to those who "walk in the light" (1 John 1:7). As long as a child of God walks in the light he can have absolute assurance in his salvation!

Examples

There are examples of actual people who fell away in the New Testament. Hymenaeus, Alexander, Philetus, and Demas are all identified as having fallen from grace (1 Timothy 1:19-20; 2 Timothy 2:17; 4:10). Ananias and Sapphira were members of the church at Jerusalem who were struck dead for lying to the Holy Spirit (Acts 5:1-10). What about Simon? He was a child of God who was certainly in danger of losing his soul (Acts 8:22-23). These names are etched in history as a vivid reminder that a child of God can forfeit his salvation. He can "depart from the faith" (1 Timothy 4:1).

Some advocates of "once saved, always saved" argue that a person who falls away never really believed in the first place. They say he was only a pretender. However, Jesus made a statement that destroys this argument. In the parable of the sower, He said, "And the ones on the rock are those who, when they hear the word, receive it with joy. But these have no root; they believe for a while, and in time of testing fall away" (Luke 8:13). Notice that they "believe" and then "fall away." No one can say that they did not really believe, for Jesus said they did! Hence, this argument is proven erroneous. Furthermore, the Israelites are another example of believers who fell away. The Bible says they "believed in the Lord" (Exodus 14:31). Yet thousands of them later fell (1 Corinthians 10:8). Do not be deceived by such arguments.

Jesus gave a parable to illustrate the nature of God's forgiveness (Matthew 18:23-35). In so doing, He clearly taught that one can fall from grace. He spoke of a man whom the master "forgave" a large debt. However, the man later refused to forgive a fellow servant of a much smaller debt. As a result, the master reinstated the debt and had him delivered to the jailors (Gr. torturers). Hence, it is possible for those who were once forgiven to ultimately be lost.

"Fall"

Perhaps the most obvious way to determine if a child of God can fall from grace is to look at the word "fall" in Scripture. Is it there? How is it used? What does it teach? We already noted that Jesus spoke of those who "fall away" when tested (Luke 8:13). New Testament writers warned that Christians could "fall" (1 Corinthians 10:12), "fall away from grace" (Galatians 5:4), "fall away from the living God" (Hebrews 3:12), "fall by the same sort of disobed-ience" (Hebrews 4:11), "fall under condemnation" (James 5:12), etc. Furthermore, the church at Ephesus had "fallen" (Revelation 2:5). The fact that the word "fall" is used in reference to Christians settles the issue. Obviously, a child of God can fall from grace.

Questions

A child of God can lie (Colossians 3:9). What if he is a liar and never repents? Will he still be saved? The Bible says that all liars shall have their part in the lake of fire (Revelation 21:8). A child of God can also get drunk (Ephesians 5:18). What if he is a drunkard and never repents? Will he still be saved? The Bible says that drunkards will not inherit the kingdom of heaven (1 Corinthians 6:9-10). Furthermore, a child of God who refuses to provide for his house is worse than an unbeliever (1 Timothy 5:8). Will he still be saved? These are appropriate questions that need to be answered.

Peter, in graphic detail, describes the pitiful condition of those who fall from grace.

"For if, after they have escaped the defilements of the world through the knowledge of our Lord and Savior Jesus Christ, they are again entangled in them and overcome, the last state has become worse for them than the first. For it would have been better for them never to have known the way of righteousness than after knowing it to turn back from the holy commandment delivered to them. What the true proverb says has happened to them: 'The dog returns to its own vomit, and the sow, after washing herself, returns to wallow in the mire'" (2 Peter 2:20-22).

Notice that Peter spoke of those who had "escaped the defilements of the world" but are "again entangled in them and overcome." He said "the last state has become worse for them than the first," and that it was better "never to have known" than to "turn back." He then compared them to a dog returning to its own vomit and to a clean sow returning to the mud. How sad!

Saved by...	But can...
Faith	Depart from faith (1 Tim. 4:1)
Gospel	Believe gospel in vain (1 Cor. 15:2)
God	Depart from God (Heb. 3:12)
Lord	Deny the Lord (2 Pet. 2:1)
Truth	Err from the truth (Jam. 5:19)
Blood	Count blood unholy (Heb. 10:29)
Grace	Fail of the grace (Heb. 12:15)

The "once saved, always saved" doctrine is false. Christians must remain faithful to stay in favor with God and to receive a crown of life (Revelation 2:10). A child of God can fall from grace.

How Can I Find the New Testament Church?

The Lord Jesus promised to establish a church while in Caesarea Philippi. He said, "And I tell you, you are Peter, and on this rock I will build my church, and the gates of hades shall not prevail against it" (Matthew 16:18). The "rock" was the truth of Peter's confession that Jesus was the Christ, the Son of the living God (v. 16). His promise came to pass on the day of Pentecost in Acts 2.

The Lord's church was founded at Jerusalem in the first century. We can read about its establishment and expansion in the New Testament. Any church founded by someone else at some other time is without authority and — by its very nature — rivals the church built by Jesus.

This writer firmly believes that the church built by Jesus is still in existence, though it is often overshadowed by the churches of men. To find it, one must look at the various marks of identification set forth in Scripture (name, work, worship, organization, plan of salvation, etc). This task is made much easier when churches admit that they were the product of mere men long after the time of Christ. For instance, consider some quotes from notable Baptist sources:

> "The history of Baptist churches cannot be carried, by the scientific method, farther back than the year 1611, when the first Anabaptist church consisting wholly of Englishmen was founded in Amsterdam by John Smyth, the Se-Baptist. This was not, strictly speaking, a Baptist Church, but it was the direct progenitor of churches in England that a few years later became Baptist, and therefore the history begins there" (*A Short History of the Baptists*, p. 4).

"The word Baptists, as the descriptive name of a body of Christians, was first used in English literature, so far as is known, in the year 1644... There had been no such churches before, and hence there was no need of the name" (*Ibid.*, p. 3).

"The earliest instance in which this name occurs as a denominational designation, so far as my information goes, befell in the year 1644... The name Baptist was in 1644 first claimed by our people. They have claimed it ever since" (*A Question in Baptist History*, pp. 92-93).

The Baptist Church admits that mere men established it long after the time of Christ. It began in the 1600's with John Smyth. This fact alone should keep one from Baptist association. We want to be in the Lord's church of the first century, not John Smyth's church of the seventeenth century!

Other churches admit to being man-made as well. Perhaps the most obvious example is the Lutheran Church, which wears the name of its founder, Martin

Luther. What makes this even more astounding is the fact that Luther had said, "I ask that men make no reference to my name, and call themselves not Lutherans, but Christians" (*A Compend of Luther's Theology*, p. 135).

Consider this chart:

Church History	
Church of Christ	30-33 A.D.
Roman Catholic Church	606-607 A.D.
Lutheran Church	1520-1530 A.D.
Church of England	1534-1535 A.D.
Presbyterian Church	1536 A.D.
Baptist Church	1607-1611 A.D.
Methodist Church	1729-1739 A.D.
Mormon Church	1830 A.D.
Seventh-Day Adventist Church	1863 A.D.
Salvation Army	1865 A.D.
Jehovah's Witnesses	1870-1879 A.D.
Pentecostal Church	1901-1906 A.D.
Christian Church	1906 A.D.
Nazarene Church	1908 A.D.

If we truly love the Lord, we will want to be a member of the church He established in the first century. Regardless of past history, personal preference, or popular opinion, we will find and associate ourselves with the church that was divinely purposed (Ephesians 3:9-11) and purchased (Acts 20:28).

Churches that admit to being man-made should be immediately marked off the list. Churches that wear names that were not worn in the New Testament, like Methodist or Presbyterian, should be excluded as well. As we continue looking at the various marks of identification set forth in Scripture, we will finally be left with what we were looking for all along, the church of Christ.

What Is Church Discipline?

A hunter was about to shoot a bear in the woods. Just before he pulled the trigger, the bear asked, "What is it you want?" The man replied, "I want a fur coat for the winter." The bear then said, "And I want a full stomach. Let's compromise." Later, the bear got up and walked away alone. He had his full stomach and the hunter had his fur coat. That's the way spiritual compromise works. It is always one-sided. Though it may seem good at the time, the only one who truly benefits is the devil. Let's keep this in mind as we study the issue of church discipline.

Need

Discipline is sorely neglected in many churches. It is rarely discussed, hardly administered, and even the most public sins among members are ignored or tolerated. This is the result of spiritual indifference. Holiness is optional, accountability is obsolete, and cowardice rules the day. There is little concern for purity and therefore little desire to deal with impurity.

Discipline is one of the most essential responsibilities of the local church. It is crucial that the moral integrity of its members be maintained. Congregations that shirk this responsibility will erode spiritually ("a little leaven leavens the whole lump") and ultimately lose their standing with the Lord. *When discipline leaves a church, Christ leaves with it!*

We recognize the need for discipline in every other area of life, whether in the home, school, workplace, military, or society. Why then do some seem surprised, and even appalled, that discipline would exist in the church? They act as if the church has no right to require certain standards of its members, and even the most flagrant transgressions should be left alone. Compare that to 1 Corinthians 5.

God did not tolerate sin in the camp of physical Israel (Exodus 32; Numbers 25; Joshua 7), and He will not tolerate sin in the camp of spiritual Israel. That is the clear lesson of the first recorded case of church discipline in the New Testament. Ananias and Sapphira were struck dead to publicly demonstrate how seriously God views sin in the church (Acts 5:1-11). He expects us to be holy as He is holy (1 Peter 1:16).

There are two types of church discipline — formative and corrective. Formative discipline is preventive in nature, and involves teaching and training members in the way of righteousness. Corrective discipline is penalizing in nature, and involves punishing members who persist in unrighteousness. This chapter will focus primarily on the latter.

Examples

There are several examples of church discipline in the New Testament. These examples provide us with much information concerning *who* is to be disciplined, *how* they are to be disciplined, and *when* they are to be disciplined. We will look at four of them: The Offender, The Immoral, The Idle, and The Divisive.

(1) The Offender. In Matthew 18, Jesus addressed a situation in which one brother sins against another brother. He set forth a three-step process. Each step is an escalation of member involvement: alone, one or two others, the church.

The first step is for the offended brother to confront the offender privately. Jesus said, "If your brother sins against you, go and tell him his fault between you and him alone" (v. 15). One can easily see the wisdom in a private confrontation. This minimizes the injury caused by the sin and lessens the likelihood of pride becoming a factor. The purpose of going to your brother is not to run him off, but to win him back. "If he listens to you, you have gained your brother."

Whereas the offender was told to go to the offended in Matthew 5:23-24, the offended is told to go to the offender in this text. Hence, both sides should take the initiative in resolving the situation.

The second step is for the offended brother to bring witnesses. Jesus said, "But if he does not listen, take one or two others along with you" (v. 16). The witnesses are there to confirm the charge and to help plead with the offender. The principle of taking others along is rooted in the Old Testament (Deuteronomy 19:15).

The third step is for the offended brother to inform the congregation. Jesus said, "If he refuses to listen to them, tell it to the church" (v. 17). At this point the private sin becomes public, and is intended to increase the pressure on the offender to seek reconciliation. If that does not work, he is to be ostracized. "And if he refuses to listen even to the church, let him be to you as a Gentile and tax collector."

Though Jesus received both Gentiles and tax collectors, they were social outcasts. Just as Gentiles and tax collectors were shunned by their peers, the offending brother was to be shunned by his brethren. This is similar to other discipline commands: "avoid them" (Romans 16:17), "not to associate with" (1 Corinthians 5:11), "keep away from" (2 Thessalonians 3:6), "have nothing to do with him" (2 Thessalonians

3:14), "avoid such people" (2 Timothy 3:5), "have nothing more to do with him" (Titus 3:10), etc. All social contact was to cease.

This three-step process is dealing with a situation in which one brother sins against another brother. It is not the pattern for dealing with sin that is widespread or well known. Guy N. Woods put it like this:

> "Who, for example, could seriously believe that Paul, the apostle, should have contacted the incestuous man of I Cor. 5, before penning his instructions to the church regarding its obligations in the matter? Are we to suppose that he was in violation of our Lord's admonitions in Matt. 18:15-17, when he warned Timothy of Hymenaeus and Philetus because of the errors they were propagating regarding the resurrection? (I Tim. 2:15-18). And, what of his rebuke of Phygellus and Hermogenes who were responsible in turning all of the saints 'in Asia' against him? Ought he to have talked with these terrorists before

making their actions publicly known? (II Tim. 1:15)" (quoted from *The Spiritual Sword*, Vol. 35, No. 1).

Also note that the local church is to carry out its own discipline. There are no outside boards, councils, courts, synods, etc. that do it. Nor is it up to any one man (Diotrephes, 3 John 9-10). As autonomous units, each congregation is fully equipped to do this task.

(2) The Immoral. In 1 Corinthians 5, Paul addressed a situation in the church at Corinth involving a sexually immoral member. He was having relations with his father's wife (stepmother). Such conduct was "not tolerated even among pagans" (v. 1). To say that they were tolerating behavior that even the pagans would find offensive is quite a charge. The Corinthian people were notoriously wicked. In fact, those who lived in drunkenness and debauchery were said to "live like a Corinthian." Paul said that even the morally depraved pagans have higher standards than that!

The brethren were rebuked for their haughty attitude and told to expel the immoral member. Paul wrote, "And you are arrogant! Ought you not rather to mourn? Let him who has done this be removed from among you" (v. 2). The concept of removal is repeated throughout the chapter: "deliver this man to Satan" (v. 5), "cleanse out the old leaven" (v. 7), "not to associate with" (vv. 9, 11), "not even to eat with such a one" (v. 11), "purge out the evil person from among you" (v. 13).

Though in Ephesus at the time, Paul boldly "pronounced judgment on the one who did such a thing" (v. 3). The brethren were to "deliver this man to Satan for the destruction of the flesh, so that his spirit may be saved in the day of the Lord" (v. 5). This language is similar to 1 Timothy 1:20, where Hymenaeus and Alexander were "handed over to Satan that they may learn not to blaspheme." In both cases, the idea is that of being expelled from the domain of Christ (the church) and thrust into the domain of Satan (the world).

This text proves that it is not always wrong to "judge" others. Paul judged the member in Corinth to be in sin and commanded the congregation to act accordingly. Though Jesus condemned hypocritical judging in Matthew 7, He commanded righteous judging in John 7. His apostle did the latter. The brethren were no longer to "associate" with the immoral member. He was to be shunned. To emphasize the degree of separation required, Paul said that they were "not even to eat with such a one" (v. 11). All social contact was to cease.

Church discipline is limited to erring children of God. It is not for sinners in the world. If that were the case, we "would need to go out of the world" (v. 10). It is for "anyone who bears the name of brother" (v. 11). "Anyone" is all-inclusive. No one is exempt. There are no exceptions for family members or close friends. This is similar to 2 Thessalonians 3:6, where Paul said "any brother."

It is interesting to note that Paul did not address the immoral member. Rather, he directed his remarks to the congregation. That is because they were acting incorrectly. By their toleration of his sin, they had fallen into sin themselves.

According to 2 Corinthians 2, the command to discipline the immoral member was a "test" to see if they were "obedient in everything" (v. 9). They passed the test, and the man repented of his sins and was restored. Let that forever silence those who say that church discipline does not work!

1 Corinthians 5, which provides a wealth of information concerning church discipline, can be divided into four parts: need (vv. 1-12), procedure (vv. 3-5), reason (vv. 6-8), and sphere (vv. 9-13).

(3) The Idle. In 2 Thessalonians 3, Paul addressed a situation in the church at Thessalonica involving "idle" members. They had stopped working to support themselves and became meddling freeloaders. It is clear that Paul considered such conduct disgraceful. "For we hear that some among you walk in idleness, not busy at work, but busybodies" (v. 11).

God has always expected man to work. Adam was placed in the garden to "work it and keep it" (Genesis 2:15), and the Jews were to "work" up to six days each week (Exodus 20:9). In fact, there was a saying among the Jews that "a man who does not teach his son a trade, teaches him to steal." That same work ethic should certainly exist in Christians (Ephesians 4:28; Colossians 3:23). There is no excuse for a child of God, who has the ability and opportunity to work, to be idle.

We are not told exactly why the members had stopped working. It may have been the result of a misunderstanding concerning the Lord's return. Regardless, Paul commanded them to work both in person (v. 10) and in a previous letter (1 Thessalonians 4:11; 5:14). He had also set the example by working to support himself while in their city (1 Thessalonians 2:9; 2 Thessalonians 3:8). That is what we call formative discipline.

Since they had not responded favorably to formative discipline, it was now time for corrective discipline. Paul wrote, "Now we command you, brothers, in the name of our Lord Jesus Christ, that you keep away from any brother who is walking in idleness and not in accord with the tradition that you received from us" (v. 6). To "keep away from" means not to associate with or to shun. The NKJV says "withdraw from." Rather than supporting an idle member who refused to work, the brethren were to "have nothing to do with him" (v. 14). All social contact was to cease.

The command to "keep away from" is similar to "let him be to you as a Gentile and a tax collector" (Matthew 18:17) and "not to associate with" (1 Corinthians 5:11) in the previous examples. Association was restricted in order to make the erring member "ashamed" (2 Thessalonians 3:14). However, they were not to "regard him as an enemy" (v. 15).

(4) The Divisive. In Titus 3, Paul addressed a situation in which a brother "stirs up division" (v. 10). He is not to be left alone or tolerated. Rather, he is to be warned "once and then twice" to turn from his divisive behavior. If that does not work, Christians are to "have nothing more to do with him."

Before shunning the offender in Matthew 18, Jesus said that a serious effort was to be made to win him back. The offended brother was to confront him privately, then take one or two others, and then inform the church. We see the same general principle in this text. Withdrawal is not the first step, it is the last step. First, the divisive brother is to be confronted. Then he is to be confronted again. If there is still no repentance, then he is to be shunned.

This action is necessary because "such a person is warped and sinful; he is self-condemned" (v. 11). That underscores the seriousness of the situation. His soul is in peril, and therefore drastic action is required (Mark 9:43-48). In Romans 16:17, Paul spoke of "those who cause divisions and create obstacles" with the same end result: "avoid them."

Reasons

There are many good reasons for church discipline. As one considers these reasons, he will be reminded that God's "ways" and "thoughts" are higher than ours (Isaiah 55:8-9), and he will develop a deeper sense of appreciation for the practice.

We should discipline...

1. *To restore fallen.* 1 Corinthians 5:5 says "so that his spirit may be saved in the day of the Lord." It is our goal to win the brother back (Matthew 18:15).

2. *To maintain purity.* 1 Corinthians 5:6 says "a little leaven leavens the whole

lump." It preserves the moral integrity of the congregation.

3. *To deter others.* 1 Timothy 5:20 says "so that the rest may stand in fear." It keeps us from sinning (Acts 5:11).

4. *To test faithful.* 2 Corinthians 2:9 says "that I might test you and know whether you are obedient in everything." It measures our commitment to carry out God's commands.

5. *To teach fallen.* 1 Timothy 1:20 says "that they may learn not to blaspheme."

6. *To glorify God.* Our Sovereign is honored when we obey His will.

7. *To strengthen church.* The congregation is fortified when sin is dealt with.

The reader will notice that "revenge" was not listed as a reason for church discipline. Discipline is administered to "get the brother back" and not to "get back at the brother."

Conclusion

Discipline is not optional. It is absolutely required. 2 Thessalonians 3:6 says, "Now we command you, brothers, in the name of our Lord Jesus Christ..." There is no good excuse for a church to shirk its responsibility in the matter. [For a more detailed study, see *Digression*, Erhardt Publications, 2013].

Other Books by the Author

Grace

Truth in Charts (Volumes 1 & 2)

Three Emperors

Three Deceivers

Characteristics of a Christian

10 Facts About...

Digression

Philippians

Coming to Christ

Silenced Cries

The Seven Letters

The Simple Truth

For more information about these books, visit
www.ErhardtPublications.com

Made in the USA
Middletown, DE
05 August 2017